The Official MANCHESTER CITY Annual 2010

CW00740444

Written by David Clayton
Designed by Simon Thorley

A Grange Publication

© 2009. Published by Grange Communications Ltd., Edinburgh,
under licence from Manchester City Football Club. Printed in the EU.

Photographs © Press Association Images
& Manchester City Football Club

ISBN 978-1-906211-83-7

£6.99

Contents

Introduction

WELCOME to The Official Manchester City Football Club Annual 2010!

It's an exciting time to be a City fan and we've tried to reflect this in what we believe to be our best-ever Official Man City Annual.

You'll find all the usual stuff like the Season Review, the 2010 Squad Cards and a look at the best goals of the season – and how to recreate them!

There's a City's Got Talent feature, The Big City Quiz, Spot the Ball, a Wordsearch and Crossword to keep you busy, plus plenty of other stuff we hope you'll enjoy.

All this plus news and stats on all the summer signings Mark Hughes has made, so what are you waiting for? Dig in!

David Clayton, Editor

SEASON REVIEW

THE STORY OF THE
2008/09 SEASON

A new manager, new signings and new owners – there was plenty of excitement as the Blues kicked off the 2008/09 campaign…

MARK Hughes knew he'd have to hit the ground running with so much expectation surrounding the club and City's Fair Play League qualification for the UEFA Cup meant the season kicked off exactly a month earlier than most Premier League clubs.

The only new face for the first game of the season was Brazilian striker Jo, signed for a fee believed to be in excess of £18m from CSKA Moscow, but his debut couldn't have been more low-key as the Blues were paired with part-timers EB/Streymur of the Faroe Islands. The first leg was held in Torshavn, the capital city of the Faroes and goals from Didi Hamann and Martin Petrov were enough to silence the 5,400 crowd.

The second leg was played at Barnsley's Oakwell stadium and again, City did just enough, winning 2-0, but Streymur had caused enough problems in both games to suggest the so-called minnows of European football could prove troublesome. The warning wasn't heeded and the Blues' next opponents - Danish outfit FC Midtjylland left the City of Manchester Stadium with a shock 1-0 first leg win.

The Premier League campaign began badly too, with Aston Villa's Gabriel Agbonlahor scoring a quick-fire hat-trick as City went down 4-2 at Villa Park, a game that saw Tal Ben-Haim make his debut for the Blues. But the disappointment was short-lived as West Ham were put to the sword a week later thanks to a double strike from Elano and a goal from Daniel Sturridge giving the Blues a 3-0 win – a game in which Belgian midfielder Vincent Kompany – another new signing – made his debut. ≫

SEASON REVIEW

THE STORY OF THE
2008/09 SEASON

Shaun Wright-Phillips rejoined the Blues for less than half the fee he'd left for as Hughes continued to re-build his team. Versatile Argentine defender Pablo Zabaleta was also confirmed as a new signing following his move from Spanish club Espanyol.

Back on the pitch, City left it until the last minute of the second leg in Midtjylland to score the goal that levelled the aggregate and guaranteed UEFA Cup football for another half-hour! With no further goals in extra time, the tie was settled by a penalty shoot-out and thanks to heroics by Joe

Hart it was left to Vedran Corluka to seal the victory.

With the Abu Dhabi United Group confirmed as City's new owners and Khaldoon Al Mubarak installed as the Blues' new chairman, the club had just a few hours to spend some of its new-found fortune. The team did its bit to maintain the feel-good factor by beating Sunderland 3-0 at the Stadium of Light thanks to a fantastic homecoming debut from Wright-Phillips who scored two goals. It would prove to be Vedran Corluka's last game for the club following his surprising move to Tottenham. ⟫

With just hours of the transfer deadline remaining, the Blues were involved with several rumoured multi-million pound bids for some of the biggest names in world football. David Villa, Dimitar Berbatov and Robinho were the three main targets with reports that bids for the latter pair had been accepted. Rumours swept Manchester that one of the stars was on his way and though Berbatov eventually joined Manchester United, Brazilian superstar Robinho became a City player for a staggering fee of £32,500,000.

Robinho's home debut against Chelsea ensured a full-house at the City of Manchester Stadium and he didn't disappoint firing home a 20-yard free-kick to put his new club 1-0 up, though it was Chelsea who triumphed 3-1 on the day. Wins over AC Omonia and a 6-0 thrashing of Portsmouth followed, but a Carling Cup defeat at Brighton (on penalties) and a 2-1 reverse at Wigan ended September in disappointing fashion.

The Blues' only League win during October came courtesy of a Robinho hat-trick against Stoke and while progression to the UEFA Cup group stages was confirmed at the start of the month, City threw a 2-0 lead over Liverpool away with Rafa Benitez's side eventually winning 3-2. »

SEASONREVIEW2008/09

It was proving to be a strange Premier League season with more than a dozen teams separated by just a few points – one victory could take you up five or six places in the table while a defeat could see a team plummet towards the bottom three. A draw at struggling Newcastle, a 2-0 defeat at Middlesbrough and a third poor performance in a row during a 2-0 loss at Bolton saw City drop into the lower half of the table for the first time. The misery continued domestically with a 2-2 draw at Hull City and a 2-1 home defeat to Spurs. But just when it looked as though the chips were down, City pulled off impressive back-to-back wins over Arsenal and Schalke before suffering a home derby loss to Manchester United – it was rollercoaster stuff!

December saw just one win in seven games including defeats at home to Everton and away to Real Racing and a 2-1 defeat to bottom-of-the-table West Brom which actually dumped the Blues into the bottom three. Mark Hughes needed his team to start producing the goods and, finally, they did with a sparkling

5-1 Boxing Day win over Hull City - particularly memorable for Hull boss Phil Brown's half-time pitch-rant!

In the New Year Craig Bellamy, Nigel de Jong and Shay Given signed for the Blues for combined fees in excess of £30m. By that time, City had crashed out of the FA Cup, losing 3-0 at home to Championship side Nottingham Forest. A 1-0 win over Wigan Athletic proved the defeat to Forest to be no more than a blip and Bellamy and de Jong then made their debuts in the 2-1 win over Newcastle United. Bellamy's pace added a new dimension to the City attack and he scored on his debut to cap a fine performance against his former club.

February was inconsistent, with only an aggregate win over FC Copenhagen keeping the Blues' hopes of silverware alive – though a 1-1 draw at Liverpool is worthy of mention.

The players of the season were proving to be Stephen Ireland, Nedum Onuoha and Shaun Wright-Phillips. Richard Dunne had re-discovered his form of old and Shay Given was showing why he is rated as one of the best keepers in the Premier League.

March saw three home wins

and three away defeats with one of the losses resulting from a penalty shoot-out – the third of the campaign. After beating Aalborg comfortably at home in the UEFA Cup, the Blues conceded two goals in the last few minutes of the second leg in Denmark to take the tie into extra time and then penalties – it was nerve-racking stuff! Two saves from Given ensured progression into the last 16 of the competition and City fans continued to dream of the final in Istanbul.
In the League, a cracking 2-0 win over Aston Villa and a hard-fought 1-0 win over Sunderland made up for successive 1-0 losses in London to West Ham and Chelsea. With City hovering around mid-table and with little chance of finishing in the top seven, it appeared winning the UEFA Cup would be the only way of qualifying for Europe next season. The Blues had lost eight and drawn twice since their epic win in Schalke back in November. Now they had to return to Germany where they faced Hamburg for a place in the UEFA Cup semi-final.

City got off to the perfect start with a goal from Ireland after just 35 seconds, but Hamburg came back strongly and equalised a few minutes later and two more goals gave Martin Jol's side a healthy lead of 3-1 to take back to Manchester.
The Blues' Europa League hopes were finally dashed when Euro hopefuls Fulham came from behind to record a third win in four years at the City of Manchester Stadium. **»**

If the City fans were downcast, however, there was no need to be. Without a doubt, the best match of the season was the second leg against Hamburg and despite the Germans taking a 1-0 lead on the night and a 4-1 aggregate lead, City produced a stirring fightback with some of the best football seen in many years during a compelling performance that had the City of Manchester Stadium rocking.

Goals from Elano and Felipe Caicedo had put City within an ace of turning the tie on its head – Elano even struck the bar twice, but despite intense pressure and numerous chances, the third goal just wouldn't come. Hamburg clung on to move into the semis while the Blues pondered about what might have been. It had been a fantastic adventure but it was over, though not before the City players received a rousing reception from the fans.

It would have been easy to let the disappointment of that result see a flat end to the season, but three successive wins against West Brom, Everton and Blackburn saw City making an unlikely late bid for seventh spot, but a 2-1 defeat at Spurs finally ended all hope. Caicedo's goal against Bolton on the final day ended the campaign on a high and secured a tenth-place finish for the Blues with the promise of much better things to come…

2008/2009
Playerofthe Year
Stephen Ireland

CITY'S star midfielder reveals the secrets behind his fantastic season with the Blues in our exclusive Q&A

Stephen, you had to fight for your right to be in the team following the arrival of several new players during the summer of 2008 ...
SI: "I felt like I had a mountain to climb to prove myself. But I didn't mind that – I was up for the challenge and I like turning up for training every day really hungry. The gaffer had a big squad and he was just finding everybody out. There were a lot of people in the same category as me. But I knew from the way I was training and the way I performed in friendlies that it was just a matter of time."

When you were left out of Mark Hughes' team during pre-season, what were your thoughts?
SI: "I got my chance against West Ham and I felt that was going to be my chance to stay in the team. I set up two or three goals, got man of the match and I thought that hopefully, it would kick-start my season – and it did and though there were numerous highs, I'm not really happy with my season as a whole. It could have been a lot, lot better. But there's more to come. Fans come up to me and say 'well done' or 'great season' but they haven't seen anything yet and I want to keep that mentality."

What's it like playing alongside players like Elano and Robinho?
SI: "I've got the confidence and ability to play alongside players of that calibre and you want to play with the best because it brings out the best in you. We're on the same wavelength. Sometimes I just set off and I know the ball's going to arrive in my stride. It's clicked quite well. Robinho and Elano are typical Brazilians – full of ability. It's a pleasure to play with them and I've learned a lot from them both."

You've committed your long-term future to City, haven't you?
SI: "Yes, I have because I'm settled here, I love the club, love the fans, and I don't see what's ever going to make me leave this club. These are very exciting times, and it's going to be interesting just to see what the line-up will be at the start of next season and how far we can push on. Hopefully we can be competing for the title and get back into Europe."

What are your targets for 2010?
SI: "In five years we can be anywhere we want to be. Every player here is ambitious, so are the manager and staff. We've set targets and we are all excited to see where we can go. Everything is developing, and it's going to continue improving. I've set myself a lot of tasks and targets for my career. I want to win trophies with City and I'd love personal awards,"

You didn't win the PFA Young Player of the Year Award, despite many people feeling you should have been the winner – but you did win the City supporters' Player of the Year....
SI: "I was shocked to be nominated for the PFA award. I didn't think I was anywhere near that level. It was great to be nominated but it's more important that the club pushes on next season. I will have the same mentality going into the 2009/10 campaign as I did in the previous one. You are only ever as good as your last game!"

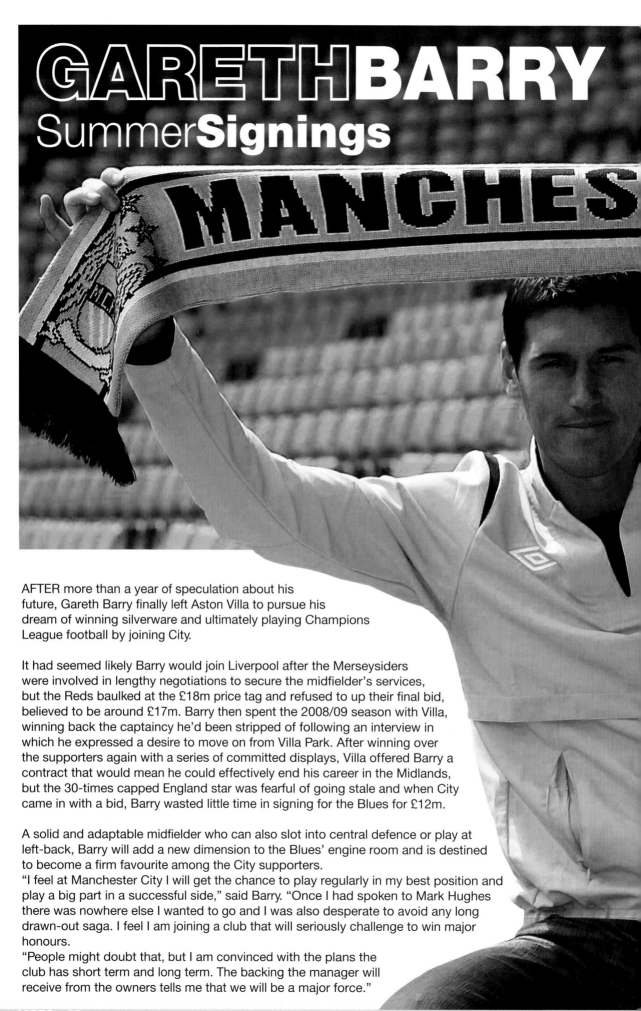

GARETH BARRY
Summer Signings

AFTER more than a year of speculation about his future, Gareth Barry finally left Aston Villa to pursue his dream of winning silverware and ultimately playing Champions League football by joining City.

It had seemed likely Barry would join Liverpool after the Merseysiders were involved in lengthy negotiations to secure the midfielder's services, but the Reds baulked at the £18m price tag and refused to up their final bid, believed to be around £17m. Barry then spent the 2008/09 season with Villa, winning back the captaincy he'd been stripped of following an interview in which he expressed a desire to move on from Villa Park. After winning over the supporters again with a series of committed displays, Villa offered Barry a contract that would mean he could effectively end his career in the Midlands, but the 30-times capped England star was fearful of going stale and when City came in with a bid, Barry wasted little time in signing for the Blues for £12m.

A solid and adaptable midfielder who can also slot into central defence or play at left-back, Barry will add a new dimension to the Blues' engine room and is destined to become a firm favourite among the City supporters.

"I feel at Manchester City I will get the chance to play regularly in my best position and play a big part in a successful side," said Barry. "Once I had spoken to Mark Hughes there was nowhere else I wanted to go and I was also desperate to avoid any long drawn-out saga. I feel I am joining a club that will seriously challenge to win major honours.

"People might doubt that, but I am convinced with the plans the club has short term and long term. The backing the manager will receive from the owners tells me that we will be a major force."

Name: Gareth Barry **Born:** 23/02/1981
Birthplace: Hastings, East Sussex **Position:** Midfielder

INFORMATIONDOWNLOAD:
CAREER HIGHLIGHTS:

- Signed by Brighton & Hove Albion as schoolboy
- Controversially joins Aston Villa as trainee in 1997 - Brighton demanded £2.5m for release of Barry and another Brighton player, Michael Standing
- FA tribunal panel rules Villa would have to pay a total sum of £2.4m dependent upon England appearances by either player
- Captains England Under-16s
- Signs first professional contract with Villa in 1998
- Makes debut for Villa versus Sheffield Wednesday as a central defender
- Makes England Under-18 debut against Bulgaria in Israel in October 1998
- England Under-21 debut versus Czech Republic
- FA Cup runner-up in 2000
- Midlands Young Player of the Year 2000 by The Football Writers Association
- Senior England debut versus Ukraine in 2000
- Intertoto Cup winner with Aston Villa
- Becomes Villa skipper
- Aston Villa Player of the Season 2006/07 and Players' Player of the Season
- In October 2007 Barry becomes youngest player to reach 300 Premier League games for Villa aged 26 years 247 days versus Bolton Wanderers
- Scores first international goal versus Trinidad and Tobago
- Barry signs five-year deal with City for a fee of £12m after 440 appearances for Villa and 52 goals

Wordsearch

GET your pen ready and look at the Wordsearch grid below – can you spot the surnames of 11 City players? Remember, the words could be written in any direction!

```
Y N A P M O K C T T L W
H B L B A R R Y X W K R
O K K L G I V E N N N C
D O L R N M H T B M D P
E Y N F V G P O Z N L C
C E M U N Y J H A P N H
I V G O O I L L B B G N
A T J D N H E L A L R I
C E R O I R A G L Z P B
D F V Z I R K R E C T C
R W Y M M T B Q T L J F
L V X K Z H M Z A C V M
```

Answers on page 60/61

Who Said It?

READ the quotes below and see if you can work out who was speaking – add a bonus point if you can also work out what they were talking about…

1. "I have been surprised at all the speculation, because I have always been consistent with everyone on the subject of the manager. Every time I have spoken, I have said that we have the highest confidence in Mark, and I would like to reiterate that now. Mark will be our manager next season - nothing has changed."

2. "We would have loved to be back in Europe but that's not going to be the case, unfortunately. Looking further ahead, maybe it is a blessing, although it doesn't feel like that at the moment because we are all disappointed that we are not going to be involved. But maybe in certain games this year, we have travelled into Europe on Thursdays then come back to play a League game on Sunday and not performed. It's happened on occasion."

3. "As a team, I'd have loved to have won the title. Unfortunately that was not possible this season, but hopefully we can do it next year. Our aim is to be champions over the next couple of years, to give our supporters the happiness they deserve."

4. "I don't think it is anything to do with the fact that he is playing so far away from home because Maradona was about 300-yards from our training ground earlier in the year and didn't pop in which was a bit of a surprise, but he is still a young player and his time will come."

5. "I have shown my commitment to Wales by turning up for these sorts of games, but it is me that always seems to get picked on for stick. I'm the one who turns up for games. I'm passionate about my country - maybe too passionate."

6. "I would love to play at City for the next 10 or 15 years. I want to be a one-club man."

7. "Where do I see City in 10 years' time? A respected club, one that every player will want to play for. Hopefully by then the club will have won many titles, such as the Premier League and Champions League. Our objective is to be big but we must work hard. We can be bigger by winning titles."

8. "I think it is going to be incredible over the next couple of years. It's not just for me, you speak to anyone in the Premier League and they would want to come to Manchester City."

9. "I have heard about the intensity of the work they do at City and I have spoken to Mark Hughes about it. I like that approach because I am a training animal."

10. "The training ground should be a working place. It is our football factory. Most people are not allowed to see their mates when they are working in a factory, so why should they come into ours? That is the idea behind it."

Answers on page 60/61

WHICH of these crackers was your personal favourite? Try and think about the technique the players used and see if you can score a similar goal in your back garden or in the park...

SIX SH

SCORER: ROBINHO
VERSUS: ARSENAL
SKILL USED: DISGUISED LOB

THE GOAL: Shaun Wright-Phillips drove forward and slid the ball through to Robinho who advanced towards goal. As Manuel Almunia left his line to narrow the angle, Robinho looked up before cleverly lifting the ball over Almunia's head and into the net.
PRACTICE: Running towards a goal and scooping the ball up and over the advancing (or imaginary) keeper.

SCORER: JAVIER GARRIDO
VERSUS: LIVERPOOL
SKILL USED: CURLING SHOT WITH PACE

THE GOAL: After Shaun Wright-Phillips was fouled outside Liverpool's penalty area, Javier Garrido strode up to take the free-kick. Most people expected him to cross the ball to the back post, but instead he clipped an exquisite curling shot into the top corner of Pepe Reina's goal and into the net.
PRACTICE: Take free-kicks from either side of the edge of the penalty area with as much pace, power and lift as possible.

SCORER: ROBINHO
VERSUS: WEST BROM
SKILL USED: VOLLEY

THE GOAL: Stephen Ireland burst into West Brom's half before spotting Robinho's run into the box. Ireland hit a perfectly-weighted ball into the Brazilian's path and City's No.10 didn't make any mistake with a rasping volley past the Albion keeper Scott Carson.
PRACTICE: Get a team-mate to throw the ball towards the six-yard box while you run in and hit a volley into the goal. Try and time your run so the ball is around knee-height when you shoot.

SCORER: PABLO ZABALETA
VERSUS: WIGAN
SKILLS USED: CONTROL AND VOLLEY

THE GOAL: Paul Scharner cleared Danny Sturridge's cross to the edge of the Wigan box into the path of Pablo Zabaleta. The Argentine defender controlled the ball before hitting a swerving half-volley past Chris Kirkland and into the net.

PRACTICE: Get a friend to throw the ball to you at chest height – then, after controlling the ball, hit it on the half-volley from about 20 yards out.

SCORER: ELANO
VERSUS: WEST HAM
SKILLS USED: TIMING & CLINICAL FINISH

THE GOAL: Elano had already scored for City after Stephen Ireland had cut to the goal-line and crossed the ball for the Brazilian to sweep home. The same pair combined to put City 2-0 up not long after: Ireland again burst to the by-line, looked up and sent in a low cross for Elano to volley home from seven yards.

PRACTICE: Get a friend to run into the box towards you and head to the edge of the six-yard box. As they near the goal-line, make your run from the edge of the area and see if you can finish their cross first time – it's all in the timing!

SCORER: STEPHEN IRELAND
VERSUS: SCHALKE
SKILLS USED: VISION & CONTROL

THE GOAL: It was Ireland who began and finished this move with a fantastic 40-yard pass out to the left where Robinho controlled the ball and waited for support. Ireland kept running and connected with Robinho's perfectly-weighted cross to slot the ball past the Hamburg goalkeeper and into the net.

PRACTICE: Start at the halfway line, play a pass out to your team-mate and make your run into the box. Get them to hold the ball for five seconds as you make your run and then cross it low towards the penalty spot for you to side-foot home.

THERE is a new batch of young stars on the brink of fame and fortune who are waiting to impress Mark Hughes and his coaches during 2009/10 – here are some of the names to look out for this season

CITY'S GOT T★LENT!

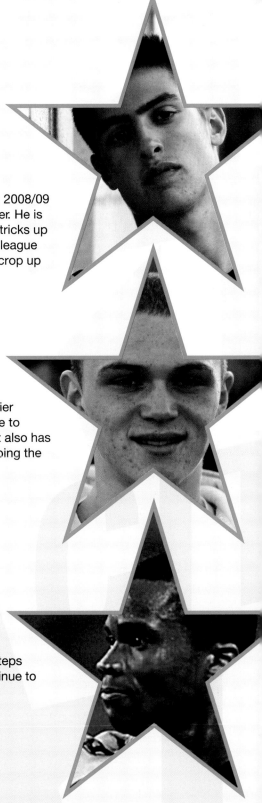

NAME: ROBBIE MAK
DATE OF BIRTH: 13/06/1990
NATIONALITY: SLOVAKIAN
POSITION: STRIKER

With 27 goals in all competitions, Robbie Mak enjoyed a superb 2008/09 season and has done his long-term chances no harm whatsoever. He is adding bulk to his frame and is a fast, direct forward with a few tricks up his sleeve. Expect him to broaden his experience in the reserve league in 2009/10 and, as a natural-born goal-scorer, his name should crop up often as the campaign progresses.

NAME: KIERAN TRIPPIER
DATE OF BIRTH: 19/09/1990
NATIONALITY: ENGLISH
POSITION: RIGHT-BACK

A key member of the FA Youth Cup-winning squad, Kieran Trippier is already an England Under-19 international and a familiar name to City fans. The Bury-born teenager is tenacious in the tackle, but also has a natural attacking flair and he likes nothing better than overlapping the midfielders to provide support in attack.

NAME: ALEX NIMELY-TCHUIMENI
DATE OF BIRTH: 11/05/1991
NATIONALITY: LIBERIAN
POSITION: STRIKER

Alex Nimely-Tchuimeni enjoyed a prolific partnership with Robbie Mak during the 2008/09 Academy campaign, finishing with 17 goals and enhancing his reputation as a talent to keep a close eye on. Nimely-Tchuimeni hails from Liberia, the country that gave the world former City striker George Weah – big footsteps to follow in! Don't be surprised to see the teenage forward continue to impress as he begins to train with the senior squad this season.

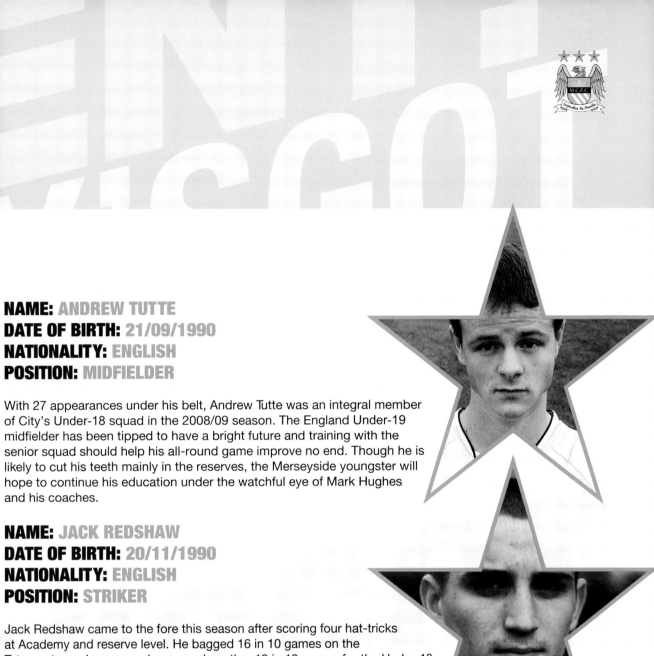

NAME: ANDREW TUTTE
DATE OF BIRTH: 21/09/1990
NATIONALITY: ENGLISH
POSITION: MIDFIELDER

With 27 appearances under his belt, Andrew Tutte was an integral member of City's Under-18 squad in the 2008/09 season. The England Under-19 midfielder has been tipped to have a bright future and training with the senior squad should help his all-round game improve no end. Though he is likely to cut his teeth mainly in the reserves, the Merseyside youngster will hope to continue his education under the watchful eye of Mark Hughes and his coaches.

NAME: JACK REDSHAW
DATE OF BIRTH: 20/11/1990
NATIONALITY: ENGLISH
POSITION: STRIKER

Jack Redshaw came to the fore this season after scoring four hat-tricks at Academy and reserve level. He bagged 16 in 10 games on the Totesport.com League and managed another 12 in 12 games for the Under-18s – that's 28 goals from 22 starts. Redshaw is likely to be a key figure as the young Blues attempt to win back the FA Youth Cup this season and the signs are he is one of the most instinctive strikers City have had in many years.

NAME: VLADIMIR WEISS
DATE OF BIRTH: 11/11/1989
NATIONALITY: SLOVAKIAN
POSITION: WINGER

City fans caught a glimpse of exciting winger Vladimir Weiss on the final day of the 2008/09 Premier League season when the Academy graduate made his senior debut against Bolton Wanderers. A key member of the FA Youth Cup-winning side of 2008, Weiss has served his apprenticeship with the reserves and is now pressing for a regular place on the City bench – if his cameo against Bolton is anything to go by, we'll see plenty more of Weiss in 2009/10.

BIGCITYQUIZ!

1 WHAT IS MAN CITY MANAGER HUGHES' FIRST NAME?

2 WHO WAS THE MANAGER WHO GAVE HIS TEAM A TELLING OFF AT HALF-TIME - ON THE CITY OF MANCHESTER STADIUM PITCH!

3 ARE CITY'S NEW SHIRT SPONSORS ETIHAD A) A SPORTS COMPANY, B) AN AIRLINE OR C) A NEWSPAPER?

4 WHO DID VLADIMIR WEISS MAKE HIS DEBUT AGAINST? A) BOLTON B) STOKE C) HULL

5 SHAY GIVEN ONCE PLAYED FOR SWINDON TOWN. TRUE OR FALSE?

6 THREE DIFFERENT CITY PLAYERS SCORED PENALTIES IN PREMIER LEAGUE GAMES DURING 2008/09 – WHO WERE THEY?

7 WHICH OF THESE CLUBS DID JOE HART NOT PLAY ON LOAN FOR – LEEDS UNITED OR BLACKPOOL?

8 THREE PLAYERS SCORED IN THREE SUCCESSIVE GAMES LAST SEASON – WHO WERE THEY?

9 WHO SCORED CITY'S FASTEST GOAL LAST SEASON?

10 WHICH COUNTRY DO BOTH VLADIMIR WEISS AND ROBBIE MAK COME FROM?

11 WHEN WAS CITY'S ACADEMY FORMED? A) 1994 B) 1998 C) 2000

12 CAN YOU NAME THE TWO TEAMS CITY BEAT ON PENALTIES IN SEASON 2008/09?

13 WHICH TEAM DID VEDRAN CORLUKA JOIN IN AUGUST 2008?

14 WHICH CITY PLAYER SCORED ON HIS SENIOR DEBUT FOR WALES?

15 BRIGHTON BEAT CITY ON PENALTIES IN THE CARLING CUP – BY WHAT SCORE?

16 WHERE DID THE BLUES PLAY THEIR FIRST HOME FIXTURE OF THE 2008/09 CAMPAIGN?

17 HOW MANY PENALTIES DID ELANO SCORE IN THE 2008/09 SEASON?

18 HOW MANY PENALTIES WERE CITY AWARDED IN TOTAL IN THE 2008/09 SEASON?

19 WHICH SIDE DID FELIPE CAICEDO JOIN CITY FROM?

20 UP TO THE END OF THE 2008/09 SEASON, WHO HAD SCORED THE MOST CAREER GOALS FOR CITY?

21 HOW MANY UEFA CUP TIES DID CITY PLAY IN SEASON 2008/09? A) 10 B) 13 C) 16

22 WHO DID TAL BEN-HAIM SPEND MOST OF HIS TIME ON LOAN WITH IN 2008/09?

23 SHAY GIVEN KEPT SIX CLEAN SHEETS FOR CITY DURING THE 2008/09 SEASON. TRUE OR FALSE?

24 HOW MANY TIMES WAS RICHARD DUNNE SENT OFF DURING 2008/09?

25 WHICH BRAZILIAN STAR DID ROBINHO GROW UP WITH? A) ELANO B) KAKA C) DIEGO

26 WHICH COUNTRY COULD NEDUM ONUOHA AND KELVIN ETUHU BOTH HAVE REPRESENTED?

27 HOW MANY OWN GOALS DID OPPOSING PLAYERS SCORE FOR CITY IN THE 2008/09 SEASON?

28 WHICH TEAM WAS PABLO ZABALETA SENT OFF AGAINST IN SEASON 2008/09?

29 CITY ONLY FAILED TO SCORE HOME AND AWAY AGAINST ONE PREMIER LEAGUE TEAM IN THE 2008/09 SEASON – WHO WAS IT?

30 WHO DID BENJANI SCORE HIS ONLY PREMIER LEAGUE GOAL AGAINST IN 2008/09?

SCOREBOARD

`87:04`

90 POINTS	**YOU'RE A GENIUS AND CAN WRITE NEXT YEAR'S QUIZ!**
75+ POINTS	**EXCELLENT EFFORT – SIGN A NEW DEAL IMMEDIATELY!**
60+ POINTS	**VERY GOOD EFFORT**
45+ POINTS	**GOOD EFFORT**
30+ POINTS	**NOT BAD AT ALL – COULD DO BETTER, THOUGH!**
15-30 POINTS	**GOOD TRY BUT NO MEDALS ON THIS OCCASION!**
LESS THAN 15	**AS SIR ALAN SUGAR SAYS, "PACK YOUR BAGS - YOU'RE FIRED!"**

Answers on page 60/61

SummerSignings
KOLOTOURE

Name: Kolo Habib Toure
Born: 19/03/1981
Birthplace:
Bouake, Ivory Coast
Position: Defender

THE Ivorian defender is quick, adaptable, excellent in the air and able to time his tackles to perfection. When it comes to consistently dependable Premier League defenders, Kolo Toure's name features somewhere near the top of most people's list - is it any wonder that Arsenal boss Arsène Wenger made Toure his defensive rock for seven years and eventually handed him the captain's armband? With a wealth of experience at the top end of English football plus eight years' worth of Champions League football, Mark Hughes didn't hesitate at paying around £14m to bring the player to the City of Manchester Stadium.

Toure was born and raised in the Ivory Coast city of Bouake and his ability at football soon attracted the attention of local side Mimosas. There he progressed at such a rate that he was handed an international debut for Ivory Coast against Rwanda aged just 19. His younger brothers Yaya and Ibrahim would both follow in his footsteps in later years, too.

After winning two league titles with Mimosas, the 21-year-old Toure was handed a trial with Arsenal in February 2002 and was soon snapped up for just £150,000. He was initially deployed as an attacking midfielder after making his debut for the Gunners during the 2002 FA Community Shield victory over Liverpool.
Wenger continued to experiment with Toure, alternating him between midfield and right-back for a time but it wasn't until the start of the 2003/04 campaign that Toure was played in central defence, partnering Sol Campbell. Soon the pair forged an understanding that became the bedrock of Arsenal's Premier League and FA Cup-winning side.

Throughout his time in England he has been a permanent fixture in the Ivory Coast national side and in 2006, Toure was part of a team that finished runners-up in the African Cup of Nations. Later that year he scored the only goal of the Champions League semi-final against Villarreal – the last European goal ever scored at Highbury - to send Arsenal to their first final where they would ultimately lose to Barcelona.

The following year, Toure represented Ivory Coast at the World Cup finals for the first time and his performances ensured there was a new four-year deal waiting for him on his return to the Emirates Stadium.

Toure was a hugely popular player among the Arsenal supporters who loved his dedication, power and attitude on the pitch and at the time of signing his contract, the player admitted he would be happy to remain a Gunner for the remainder of his career. He wore the club captain's armband for the first time during a dramatic 6-3 Carling Cup victory over Liverpool in 2007, but his career in North London was about to take a blow.

In 2008 Toure contracted malaria following a summer break in his native Ivory Coast, laying him low for several weeks before he made a full recovery from an illness that is all too common in Africa.

After City unsuccessfully bid for the player during the January 2009 transfer window, Blues boss Hughes returned with an offer that was acceptable to all parties and the former Gunners star followed in the footsteps of ex-team-mate and friend Emmanuel Adebayor by joining City and penning a four-year deal in July 2009.

"City showed that they really want me and I'm wholly happy," said Kolo after completing his move north. "They have given me the love and I'm really delighted to bring them back the love. The quality is big, there are fantastic players here. I will give everything I have to make the club one of the best in England.

INFORMATIONDOWNLOAD:
CAREER HIGHLIGHTS:

- Older brother of Barcelona midfielder Yaya Toure and Al-Ittihad striker Ibrahim Toure
- Begins youth career with Ivorian side Mimosas
- April 2000: Makes international debut for Ivory Coast vs. Rwanda
- 2002: Signs for Arsenal for £150,000
- August 2002: Makes debut for the Arsenal first team against Liverpool in the FA Community Shield
- May 2003: FA Cup Winner

- 2003-04: Part of the title-winning Arsenal squad that goes entire season without losing a Premier League game
- May 2005: FA Cup winner
- 2006: Runner up in African Cup of Nations with Ivory Coast
- June 2006: Makes first appearance in a World Cup game vs. Argentina
- January 2007: Captains Arsenal for the first time in a Carling Cup victory over Liverpool - Arsenal won 6-3

Who Is Celebrating?

WE'VE disguised the four goalscorers below - can you work out who is celebrating beneath the bubblewrap?

Answers on page 60/61

Crossword

TEST your knowledge of the Blues by answering the questions below and filling in our crossword puzzle...

ACROSS

1 Name of the 2009/10 shirt sponsor? (6)
6 City's first 2009 summer signing? (6,5)
8 Club Robinho signed from? (4,6)
10 The Blues faced three teams from this country during the 2008/09 UEFA Cup run? (7)
11 Vladimir Weiss was born in this country? (8)
13 Team that knocked City out of the 2008/09 UEFA Cup? (7)
15 Ireland's Number One? (4,5)
17 Team Jo joined on loan in 2009? (7)
18 Mark Hughes' nickname? (6)
19 Which country does Craig Bellamy captain? (5)

DOWN

1 Who does Felipe Caicedo represent at international level? (7)
2 Former Chelsea full-back who joined City in January 2009? (5,6)
3 Country Nedum Onuoha was born in? (7)
4 Dutch midfielder who signed from Hamburg? (5,2,4)
5 Team that knocked City out of the Carling Cup? (8)
7 Surname of striker who played for Juventus and Fiorentina? (7)
9 Only player to score a hat-trick for the Blues last season? (7)
12 Team that knocked City out of the FA Youth Cup last season? (7)
14 City's kit manufacturer for the 2009/10 season? (5)
16 City player whose surname is also a country? (7)

Answers on page 60/61

Autograph!

EVERYBODY has a hero or a favourite player they model themselves on – and professional footballers are no different. Here are the players the City stars used to idolise as kids…

1: JOE HART:

"David Seaman when he was at Arsenal – he was a legend. I never managed to get his autograph, though I did get a few Shrewsbury Town players as a kid."

2: NEDUM ONUOHA:

"I'm not really one to have heroes as such, but a player I remember admiring when I was young was George Weah. I used to watch Gazetta Football Italia every week on Channel Four. I used to love Italian football at the time. I remember that goal he scored when he ran the length of the pitch all on his own, plus he later came to City."

3: ROBINHO:

"On the pitch it is Ronaldo – off it, it is my father. The first autograph I asked for was Pele, who was training the youth team at Santos – he is a very nice guy."

4: ELANO:

"The first autographs I ever asked for were Roberto Carlos and Ronaldo and I also got Freddy Rincon of Colombia. Romario is a great inspiration to all Brazilians, too."

5: JAVIER GARRIDO:

"It was in San Sebastian after a Real Sociedad match, I asked a player named Jose Pikabea to sign my programme. I was about 15 at the time."

6: MICHAEL JOHNSON:

"It was Gary McAllister when he was at Leeds United, the club I supported as a boy. I remember having his name on my shirt. My first autograph was Carlton Palmer, also when he was at Leeds. I got it when he came out of Elland Road after a match but I've only got vague memories of it"

7: PABLO ZABALETA:

"There was an Argentinian player called Bochini who I spotted while in a shopping centre so I asked for his autograph and he was happy to pose for a photograph with me and my friends – I was 12 at the time!"

8: STEPHEN IRELAND:

"I was at the Bobby Charlton Soccer School when I was 11 and I met my childhood hero Eric Cantona there and asked for his autograph – I was completely star-struck!"

Young and in love.

LIVE4CITY is the FREE seasonal membership for all fans who love City. Join up for access to great benefits such as match tickets for £5 and your chance to train at our Platt Lane Academy.

Sign up now at LIVE4CITY.co.uk and receive your FREE membership pack.

live4city

Summer**Signings**
EMMANUEL ADEBAYOR

Name: Sheyi Emmanuel Adebayor **Born:** 26/02/1984
Birthplace: Lomé, Togo **Position:** Striker

EMMANUEL Adebayor or 'Manu' as he is better known became a member of City's superstar strike force after deciding to quit Champions League semi-finalists Arsenal for the City of Manchester Stadium.

The Togolese striker had become hot property while with the Gunners and had been courted by Europe's top clubs for several seasons before Mark Hughes finally captured the Premier League hot-shot in a deal reportedly worth around £25million. Adebayor has come a long way from his relatively humble beginnings in Lomé where he made his first inroads into becoming an African king.

He was just 13 when he was snapped up by his hometown club Sporting Club de Lomé and within a year he was offered a trial by French side Metz, eventually joining Le Championnat in 1999, aged just 15.

After two years in the Metz academy team, both Nigeria and Togo made enquiries as to which country the promising teenager would be representing at international level. Adebayor was eligible to play for the Super Eagles, but his heart was one hundred per cent Togolese and it was his birth nation that he elected to play for.

The decision meant he'd never be able to play alongside his boyhood hero, Nigerian legend Nwankwo Kanu, but his style and quick feet earned him the ultimate accolade of being nicknamed 'baby Kanu' by his team-mates.

Aged 17 he began playing for the Metz senior side and the following season (2002/03) saw him fulfil the promise he'd shown as a kid as he knocked in goals at a rate of one every two matches.

But of course, there was much more to come from Manu. In 2003 he joined French giants Monaco and soon earned a reputation as one of France's hottest talents.

He celebrated his 21st year by scoring 11 goals in World Cup qualification for Togo – the highest total of any African player – a record that convinced Arsenal boss Arsène Wenger to offer a fee that would eventually rise to £7million to bring him to the Premier League. In joining the Gunners, Adebayor was also following in the footsteps of hero Kanu who was still held in great esteem by the Arsenal supporters.

His gangly running style and trickery proved that he had based himself on his hero and he quickly endeared himself to the supporters as he prepared to step into Thierry Henry's sizeable boots.

His record for Arsenal was prolific by Premier League standards and during the 2007/08 season he became the first player to score a hat-trick at home and away against the same team (Derby County) in the elite division.

His form won him a place in the 2008 PFA Team of the Year and the coveted Match of the Day Goal of the Season award, not to mention a fourth successive Togolese Football of the Year award. Continually linked with AC Milan during the summer of 2008, Adebayor remained with Arsenal for one more season before the Gunners accepted City's mammoth offer. The Blues' new No.25 will now forge an exciting front line that includes Roque Santa Cruz, Carlos Tevez and Robinho and he says he's come to what he believes will soon be the best team in the world – here's hoping!

INFORMATION DOWNLOAD:
CAREER HIGHLIGHTS:

- 2004: Champions League runner-up with Monaco
- 2005: Togolese Footballer of the Year
- 2006: Scores on Arsenal debut in 2-0 victory vs. Birmingham City
- 2006: Made national side captain
- 2006: Wins Togolese Footballer of the Year for second time
- 2007: Wins Togolese Footballer of the Year for third time
- 2008: Wins Togolese Footballer of the Year for fourth time
- 2009: Confederation of African Football choose Adebayor as African Player of the Year for 2008 (first ever Togolese winner)
- 2009: Signs a five-year contract with MCFC for a fee in the region of £25m

SummerSignings
CARLOSTEVEZ

Carlos Tevez joined City in July - here we look at the career of the Argentinian striker

Name: Carlos Alberto Tevez **Born:** 05/02/1984
Birthplace: Buenos Aries, Argentina **Position:** Forward

CARLOS Tevez joined a select band of players to cross the city from Manchester United to become a Manchester City player when he signed a five-year deal in July 2009. The Blues paid Tevez's owners in the region of £25m for the forward who was a cult hero at both United and West Ham. He will forge a dream front line that will include Roque Santa Cruz and Robinho and his hard-working ethic, talent and endeavour are sure to make him a huge hit with the City fans.

"My ambition is to help Manchester City recover the status they once had as one of the best clubs in Europe and to try and win trophies," explained Tevez. "The coach and the owners made me understand the reality at Manchester City - it was a very important decision for me to make but it is a bit of a strange sensation for me to be back again in Manchester," said Tevez upon signing. "I will give everything to help City become one of the biggest and most important clubs in England - and win some trophies.
"But it is very important to remember I am just one more player to add to the strength of the squad, one more player working with the coach and my new team-mates to help us win trophies for City."

Tevez has had an interesting path to the City of Manchester Stadium. He began his quest to become a famous player in 1992 when he joined local side All Boys, a junior club, aged eight.

His real name is Carlos Alberto Martinez, but he had his surname changed to that of his mother due to a dispute between All Boys and Boca Juniors, the club he eventually joined in 1997. In 2001, aged 17, he made his senior debut for the club against Talleres de Cordoba.

His progress was rapid and in 2003 he was awarded the Argentine Player of the Year award, alerting several top clubs in Europe that Boca had a player of some talent on their books.

He began his international career with Argentina in 2004 and won a gold medal at the Olympic Games that year, also winning the Golden Boot for his eight goals in six games. Before Christmas, he moved to legendary Brazilian side Corinthians for a South American transfer record of £13.7m.

After enjoying a successful spell in Brazil and becoming the first foreign player to win the Brazilian Football Confederation's Best Player award since 1976, as well as the South American Player of the Year award, he was called up to the 2006 Argentina World Cup squad. He then moved to West Ham United in a loan deal that included fellow countryman Javier Mascherano and was voted the Hammers' Player of the Year at the end of the season after scoring a dramatic winner at Manchester United to keep the club up and relegate Sheffield United. He joined United later that summer in a two-year loan deal and, just as he'd been with West Ham, quickly became a huge crowd favourite.

After two years at Old Trafford he opted to join City. Put your money on him now for City's 2009/10 Player of the Year award!

INFORMATION DOWNLOAD:
CAREER HIGHLIGHTS:

- May 2007: Scored the only goal of the final game of the season against Manchester United which ensured West Ham's safety in the Premier League
- June 2007: Tevez rejects a move to Inter Milan
- December 2007: West Ham fans welcomed Tevez back to Upton Park as part of the United squad by chanting "there's only one Carlos Tevez"
- May 2008: Wins Premier League title and European Champions' League with Manchester United
- Described by Diego Maradona as "Argentine prophet for the 21st century"
- August 2008: Winner of Community Shield
- December 2008: Wins FIFA Club World Cup
- February 2009: Wins League Cup
- July 2009: Tevez agrees five year deal with Manchester City

ROBINHO

Spot the Ball

MANCHESTER CITY FC
Squad Profiles 2010

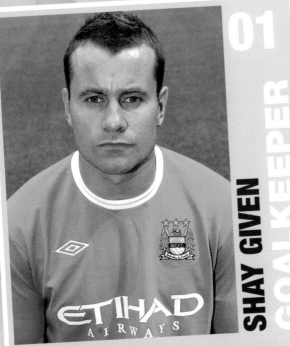

01

SHAY GIVEN GOALKEEPER

Born: 20/4/1976 **Nationality:** Irish
Previous clubs: Celtic, Blackburn Rovers, Swindon Town (loan) Sunderland (loan), Newcastle Utd
Career highlight: Becoming Ireland's most capped goalkeeper

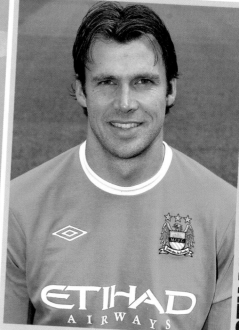

12

STUART TAYLOR GOALKEEPER

Born: 28/11/1980 **Nationality:** English
Previous clubs: Arsenal, Bristol Rovers (loan) Crystal Palace (loan) Peterborough (loan), Leicester (loan) Aston Villa, Cardiff (loan) **Career highlight:** Premier League champions medal winner

16

KASPER SCHMEICHEL GOALKEEPER

Born: 5/11/1986 **Nationality:** Danish
Previous clubs: Darlington (loan), Bury (loan), Cardiff City (loan), Coventry City (loan)
Career highlight: His display in the 1-0 win over Manchester United in 2007

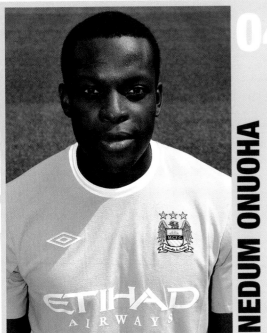

04 NEDUM ONUOHA DEFENDER

Born: 12/11/1986 **Nationality:** Nigerian
Previous clubs: None **Career highlight:**
Captaining England Under-21s

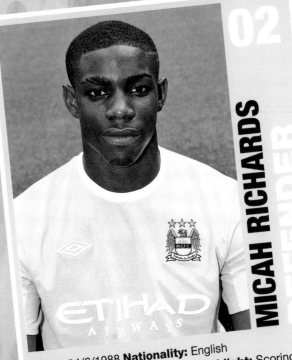

02 MICAH RICHARDS DEFENDER

Born: 24/6/1988 **Nationality:** English
Previous clubs: None **Career highlight:** Scoring
for England vs Israel at Wembley in 2007

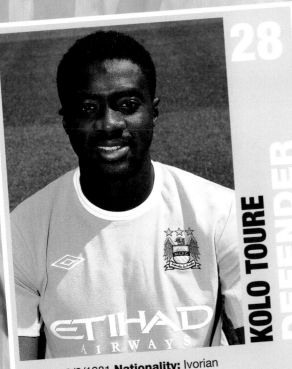

28 KOLO TOURE DEFENDER

Born: 19/3/1981 **Nationality:** Ivorian
Previous clubs: Mimosas, Arsenal
Career highlight: Playing for Ivory Coast in the
2006 World Cup

MANCHESTER CITY FC
Squad Profiles 2010

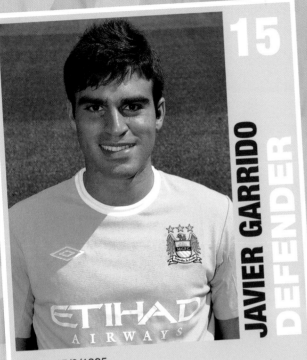

15 JAVIER GARRIDO — DEFENDER

Born: 15/3/1985
Nationality: Spanish
Previous clubs: Real Sociedad
Career highlight: Representing Spain at Under-21 level

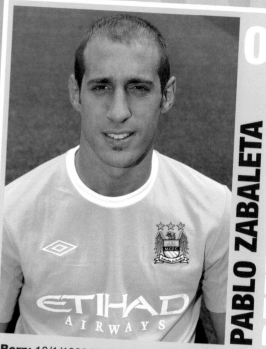

05 PABLO ZABALETA — DEFENDER

Born: 16/1/1985 **Nationality:** Argentinian
Previous clubs: San Lorenzo, Espanyol
Career highlight: Winning gold medal for Argentina at 2008 Olympics

22 RICHARD DUNNE — DEFENDER

Born: 21/9/1979 **Nationality:** Irish
Previous clubs: Everton **Career highlight:** Winning his 50th cap for Ireland and winning City's Player of the Year for four successive years

03 WAYNE BRIDGE DEFENDER

Born: 5/8/1980 **Nationality:** English
Previous clubs: Southampton, Chelsea, Fulham
(loan) **Career highlight:** Winning first England cap
vs Holland in 2002

26 TAL BEN-HAIM DEFENDER

Born: 31/3/1982 **Nationality:** Israeli
Previous clubs: Maccabi Tel Aviv, Bolton Wanderers,
Chelsea, Sunderland (loan)
Career highlight: Winning first international cap for
Israel in 2002

34 NIGEL DE JONG MIDFIELDER

Born: 30/11/1984 **Nationality:** Dutch
Previous clubs: Ajax, Hamburg
Career highlight: International debut for Holland
vs France in 2004

MANCHESTER CITY FC
Squad Profiles 2010

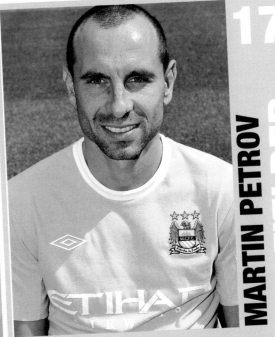

17

MARTIN PETROV MIDFIELDER

Born: 15/1/1979 **Nationality:** Bulgarian
Previous clubs: Vratsa, CSKA Sofia, Servette, VfL
Wolfsburg, Atletico Madrid **Career highlight:** Voted
Bulgarian Footballer of the Year 2006

06

MICHAEL JOHNSON MIDFIELDER

Born: 24/2/1988 **Nationality:** English
Previous clubs: None **Career highlight:** Making
England Under-21 debut

33

VINCENT KOMPANY MIDFIELDER

Born: 10/4/1986 **Nationality:** Belgian
Previous clubs: Anderlecht, Hamburg
Career highlight: International debut for Belgium
vs France in 2004 aged 18

GARETH BARRY MIDFIELDER **18**

Born: 23/2/1981 **Nationality:** English
Previous clubs: Brighton, Aston Villa
Career highlight: First England cap vs Ukraine in 2002

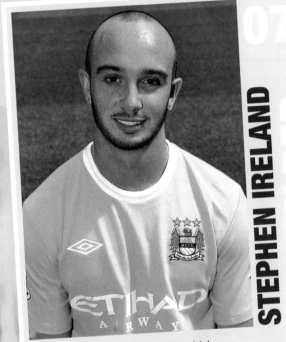

STEPHEN IRELAND MIDFIELDER **07**

Born: 22/8/1986 **Nationality:** Irish
Previous clubs: None **Career highlight:** First Ireland cap and being nominated for PFA Young Player of the Year

KELVIN ETUHU MIDFIELDER **29**

Born: 30/5/1988 **Nationality:** Nigerian
Previous clubs: Rochdale (loan), Leicester City (loan) **Career highlight:** Scoring first goal for City vs Bolton in 2007

MANCHESTER CITY FC
Squad Profiles 2010

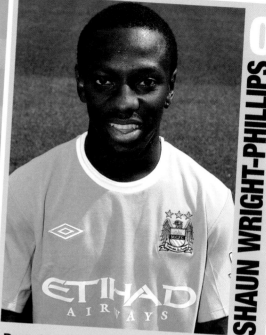

SHAUN WRIGHT-PHILLIPS — **MIDFIELDER** — 08

Born: 25/10/1981 **Nationality:** English
Previous clubs: Chelsea
Career highlight: Scoring on his England debut vs Ukraine 2004

ADAM CLAYTON — **MIDFIELDER** — 31

Born: 14/1/1989 **Nationality:** English
Previous clubs: None
Career highlight: Named as sub for City vs West Brom 2008

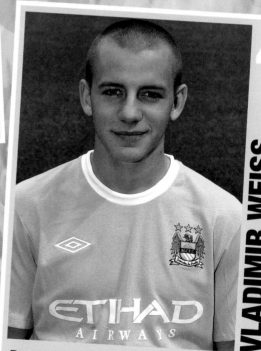

VLADIMIR WEISS — **MIDFIELDER** — 40

Born: 30/11/1989 **Nationality:** Slovakian
Previous clubs: None
Career highlight: City debut vs Bolton 2009

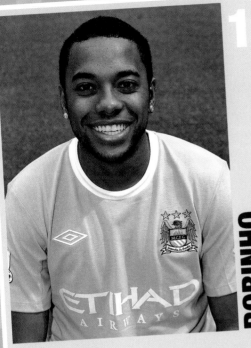

10 FORWARD

ROBINHO

Born: 25/1/1984
Nationality: Brazilian
Previous clubs: Santos, Real Madrid
Career highlight: First cap for Brazil vs Mexico in 2003

27 FORWARD

BENJANI

Born: 13/8/1978 **Nationality:** Zimbabwean
Previous clubs: Jomo Cosmos, Grasshoppers Zurich (loan), Auxerre, Portsmouth
Career highlight: Being appointed captain of Zimbabwe in 2006

39 FORWARD

CRAIG BELLAMY

Born: 13/7/1979 **Nationality:** Welsh
Previous clubs: Norwich, Coventry, Liverpool, Newcastle, Celtic (loan), Blackburn, West Ham
Career highlight: Being appointed captain of Wales in 2007

32

CARLOS TEVEZ
FORWARD

Born: 5/2/1984 **Nationality:** Argentinian
Previous clubs: Boca Juniors, Corinthians, West Ham, Manchester United **Career highlight:** Gold medal with Argentina at the 2004 Olympic Games

25

EMMANUEL ADEBAYOR
FORWARD

Born: 26/2/1984 **Nationality:** Togolese
Previous clubs: Lome, Metz, Monaco, Arsenal
Career highlight: Successive Togo Player of the Year awards 2005, 2006, 2007 & 2008. African Player of the Year 2008

14

ROQUE SANTA CRUZ
FORWARD

Born: 16/8/1981 **Nationality:** Paraguayan
Previous Clubs: Olimpia, Bayern Munich, Blackburn
Career Highlight: Voted Paraguayan Footballer of the Year in 1999. Won 61 caps for his country

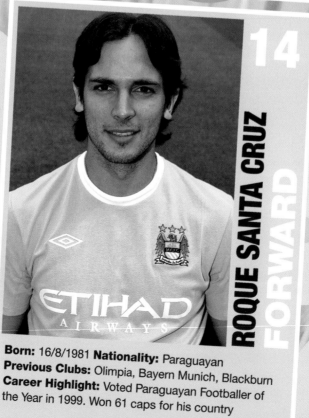

EMMANUEL ADEBAYOR

Legend (left margin): HOME | AWAY | PREMIERSHIP | CARLING CUP | FA CUP | UEFA | YELLOW CARD ✷ RED CARD | **Bold** = GOALSCORER | ELANO **P** = PENALTY SCORED | * = ESTIMATED CROWD | ★ = WON ON PENS | ○ LOST ON PENS

Month	Opponent	Att	Score	Starting Line-Up	Subs Used
JULY					
17	EB/Streymur (UEFA Q1 Leg 1)	5,400	2-0	Hart / Onuoha Richards Dunne Ball / Ireland Hamann Johnson Petrov / Vassell Jo	Evans Gelson
31	EB/Streymur (UEFA Q1 Leg 2)	7,344	2-0*	Hart / Corluka Richards Dunne Ball / Sturridge Gelson Johnson Petrov / **Vassell** Elano	Evans Hamann Etuhu
AUG					
14	**Midtjylland (UEFA Q2 Leg 1)**	17,100	0-1	Hart / Corluka Richards Dunne Ben Haim / Sturridge Gelson Johnson Petrov / Caicedo Elano	Etuhu Bojinov
17	Aston Villa	39,995	2-4	Hart / **Corluka** Richards Ben Haim Garrido / Etuhu Gelson Johnson Petrov / Evans **Elano**P	Ireland Sturridge
24	**West Ham**	36,635	3-0	Hart / Corluka Richards Ben Haim Ball / Ireland Kompany Johnson Petrov / **Elano**2 **Sturridge**	Evans Etuhu Hamann
28	Midtjylland (UEFA Q2 Leg 2)	9,460	1-0 ★	Hart / Ben Haim Richards Dunne Ball / Ireland Corluka Johnson Petrov / Elano Jo	Evans Sturridge Hamann
31	Sunderland	39,622	3-0	Hart / Ball Richards Dunne Kompany / **Ireland** Corluka Johnson **SWP**2 / Hamann Jo	Gelson Ben Haim Elano
SEPT					
13	**Chelsea**	47,331	1-3	Hart / Zabaleta Dunne Richards Ball / Kompany Hamann Ireland SWP / **Robinho** Jo	Sturridge Gelson
18	AC Omonia (UEFA 1, Leg 1)	15,000*	2-1	Hart / Zabaleta Dunne Dunne Garrido / SWP Ireland Kompany Elano / **Robinho** Jo2	Gelson Hamann Sturridge
21	**Portsmouth**	40,121	6-0	Hart / Zabaleta Richards **Dunne** Garrido / Kompany Ireland Elano **SWP** / **Robinho** Jo	**Gelson Evans** Sturridge
24	Brighton (Carling Cup 2)	8,729	2-2 ○	Schmeichel / Zabaleta Ben-Haim Dunne Ball / Kompany **Ireland** Johnson **Gelson** / Sturridge Jo	Caicedo Elano Evans
28	Wigan	18,214	1-2	Hart / Zabaleta Richards Dunne Garrido / **Kompany** Ireland Elano SWP / Robinho Jo	Gelson Evans Sturridge
OCT					
02	**AC Omonia (UEFA 1, Leg 2)**	25,304	2-1	Hart / Zabaleta Richards Ben Haim Garrido / Kompany Ireland **Elano** **SWP** / Robinho Jo	Hamann Evans Petrov
05	**Liverpool**	47,218	2-3	Hart / Zabaleta Richards Dunne **Garrido** / Kompany **Ireland** Elano SWP / Robinho Jo	Evans Petrov Gelson
20	Newcastle	45,908	2-2	Hart / Ben-Haim Richards Dunne Garrido / Kompany **Ireland** Hamann SWP / **Robinho**P Jo	Evans Onuoha Sturridge
26	**Stoke**	44,624	3-0	Hart / Ben-Haim Richards Dunne Garrido / Kompany Ireland Elano SWP / **Robinho**3 Evans	Sturridge Onuoha Gelson
29	Middlesbrough	25,731	0-2	Hart / Ben-Haim Richards Dunne Onuoha / Kompany Ireland Elano SWP / Robinho Sturridge	Evans Gelson
NOV					
02	Bolton	21,095	0-2	Hart / Ben-Haim Richards Dunne Zabaleta / Kompany Ireland Elano SWP / Robinho Evans	Sturridge Hamann
06	**FC Twente (UEFA Matchday 1)**	21,247	3-2	Hart / Zabaleta Dunne Richards Garrido / Gelson **SWP** Ireland Vassell / **Robinho** Jo	Elano **Benjani**
09	**Tottenham**	41,853	1-2	Hart / Zabaleta Dunne Richards Garrido / Gelson SWP Ireland Vassell / **Robinho** Benjani	Hamann
16	Hull	24,902	2-2	Hart / Zabaleta Ben Haim Richards Garrido / Kompany SWP **Ireland**2 Vassell / Robinho Benjani	Schmeichel Jo
22	**Arsenal**	44,878	3-0	Hart / Zabaleta Dunne Richards Garrido / Kompany SWP **Ireland** Vassell / **Robinho** Benjani	Elano Hamann **Sturridge**P
27	Schalke 04 (UEFA Matchday 2)	54,142	2-0	Hart / Kompany Dunne Richards Garrido / Hamann SWP **Ireland** Vassell / Sturridge **Benjani**	Ball Jo
30	**Man Utd**	47,320	0-1	Hart / Kompany Dunne Richards Garrido / Hamann SWP Ireland Vassell / Robinho Benjani	Elano Sturridge Zabaleta
DEC					
03	**PSG (UEFA Matchday 3)**	25,000	0-0	Hart / Kompany Dunne Zabaleta Ben Haim Garrido / Jo Ireland Vassell / Sturridge Elano	Benjani Evans
06	Fulham	24,012	1-1	Hart / Zabaleta Ben Haim Dunne Kompany Ball / SWP Ireland Vassell / **Benjani** Hamann	Evans
13	**Everton**	41,344	0-1	Hart / Zabaleta Richards Dunne Ball / Kompany SWP Ireland Elano / Robinho Benjani	Jo Vassell
18	Real Racing (UEFA Matchday 4)	21,000	1-3	Schmeichel / Zabaleta Richards Ben Haim Garrido / Hamann Gelson Elano Jo / Ireland Kompany	**Caicedo**
21	West Brom	25,010	1-2	Hart / Zabaleta Dunne Richards Ball / Kompany Gelson Ireland Vassell / Benjani SWP	**Caicedo**
26	**Hull**	45,196	5-1	Hart / Zabaleta Dunne Richards Ball / Kompany SWP **Ireland** Elano / **Robinho**2 **Caicedo**2	Onuoha Gelson Jo
28	Blackburn	25,200	2-2	Hart / Zabaleta Dunne Onuoha Ball / Kompany SWP Ireland Elano / **Robinho** Caicedo	Richards Vassell **Sturridge**
JAN					
03	Nott'm Forest (FAC3)	31,869	0-3	Hart / Zabaleta Dunne Richards Ball / Kompany SWP Gelson Elano / Sturridge Caicedo	Vassell Hamann Jo
17	**Wigan**	41,262	1-0	Hart / **Zabaleta** Dunne Richards Bridge / Kompany SWP Onuoha Elano / Sturridge Robinho	Garrido
28	**Newcastle**	42,280	2-1	Hart / Zabaleta Onuoha Richards Bridge / Kompany **SWP** Ireland De Jong / Robinho **Bellamy**	Elano Gelson Caicedo
31	Stoke	27,236	0-1	Hart / Zabaleta Onuoha Richards Bridge / Kompany SWP Ireland De Jong / Robinho Bellamy	Elano Caicedo
FEB					
07	**Middlesbrough**	40,558	1-0	Given / Zabaleta Onuoha Richards Bridge / Kompany SWP Ireland De Jong / Robinho **Bellamy**	Caicedo
14	Portsmouth	20,018	0-2	Given / Zabaleta Onuoha Logan Bridge / Kompany Elano Ireland De Jong / Robinho Bellamy	Evans Caicedo
19	FC Copenhagen (UEFA Cup R32)	30,159	2-2	Given / Zabaleta Dunne Richards Bridge / Kompany SWP **Ireland** **Onuoha** / Robinho Bellamy	Caicedo
22	Liverpool	44,259	1-1	Given / Zabaleta Onuoha Dunne Bridge / Kompany Richards Ireland De Jong / Robinho **Bellamy**	Caicedo
26	**FC Copenhagen (UEFA Cup R32)**	26,018	2-1	Given / Zabaleta Onuoha Dunne Bridge / Kompany Richards Ireland SWP / Robinho **Bellamy**2	
MAR					
01	West Ham	34,562	0-1	Given / Zabaleta Onuoha Dunne Bridge / Kompany Richards Ireland De Jong / Robinho Bellamy	Caicedo Elano Bojinov
04	**Aston Villa**	40,137	2-0	Given / Zabaleta Onuoha Dunne Bridge / Kompany **SWP** Ireland De Jong / **Elano**P Caicedo	Gelson Evans Bojinov
12	Aalborg (UEFA Cup R16) Leg 1	24,596	2-0	Given / Zabaleta Onuoha Dunne Bridge / Richards **SWP** Ireland **Caicedo** Elano / Robinho	Evans Etuhu
15	Chelsea	41,810	0-1	Given / Zabaleta Onuoha Dunne Bridge / Richards SWP Ireland Caicedo Elano / Robinho	Evans Etuhu Bojinov
19	Aalborg (UEFA Cup R16) Leg 2	10,735	0-2 ★	Given / Zabaleta Onuoha Dunne Bridge / Richards SWP Ireland Kompany Evans / Robinho	Garrido Caicedo Elano
22	**Sunderland**	43,017	1-0	Given / Zabaleta Onuoha Dunne Bridge / **Richards** SWP Elano Kompany / Robinho Bojinov	Garrido Gelson Bellamy
APR					
04	Arsenal	60,097	0-2	Given / Zabaleta Onuoha Dunne Bridge / Kompany Richards De Jong Bellamy / Robinho SWP	Gelson Sturridge Elano
09	Hamburg (UEFA Cup Q-F) Leg 1	50,000	1-3	Given / Zabaleta Onuoha Dunne Bridge / Richards SWP **Ireland** Bellamy / Robinho Sturridge	Garrido Gelson Benjani
12	**Fulham**	39,841	1-3	Given / Zabaleta Onuoha Dunne Bridge / Garrido Richards De Jong **Ireland** / Petrov Bojinov	Robinho Evans Sturridge
16	**Hamburg (UEFA Cup Q-F) Leg 2**	47,009	2-1	Given / Zabaleta Onuoha Dunne Bridge / Richards Kompany Ireland **Elano**P / **Robinho** Caicedo	Gelson Sturridge
19	**West Brom**	40,072	4-2	Given / Zabaleta **Onuoha** Dunne Bridge / Kompany De Jong Ireland **Elano**P / **Robinho** Caicedo	Gelson **Sturridge**P Petrov
25	Everton	37,791	2-1	Given / Richards Onuoha Dunne Bridge / Kompany De Jong **Ireland** Elano / **Robinho** Caicedo	Evans Gelson Petrov
MAY					
02	**Blackburn**	43,976	3-1	Given / Richards Onuoha Dunne Bridge / Kompany De Jong Ireland **Elano**P / **Robinho** Caicedo	Bojinov Petrov
10	Man Utd	75,464	0-2	Given / Richards Onuoha Dunne Bridge / Kompany De Jong Ireland Elano / Robinho Caicedo	Bojinov Petrov Evans
16	Tottenham	36,000	1-2	Given / Richards Onuoha Dunne Bridge / Kompany De Jong Ireland Elano / Petrov Caicedo	Benjani **Bojinov** Zabaleta
24	**Bolton**	47,202	1-0	Given / Richards Onuoha Dunne Bridge / Kompany De Jong Ireland SWP / Robinho **Caicedo**	Berti Weiss Zabaleta

2008/09 PLAYER STATS

Player	(Premier Lg) Apps	Goals	(Cup Comps) Goals Cup		Totals Apps	Goals
Joe Hart	23	0	10	0	33	0
Kasper Schmeichel	(0) 1	0	2	0	2 (1)	0
Shay Given	15	0	6	0	21	0
Micah Richards	28 (1)	1	15	0	43 (1)	1
Michael Ball	8	0	2 (1)	0	10 (1)	0
Nedum Onuoha	14 (3)	1	6	0	20 (1)	1
Pablo Zabaleta	25 (1)	1	12	0	37 (1)	1
Javier Garrido	11 (2)	1	6	0	17 (2)	1
Richard Dunne	25	1	15	0	40	1
Wayne Bridge	10	0	5	0	15	0
Tal Ben-Haim	8 (1)	0	6	0	14 (1)	0
Shaleum Logan	1	0	0	0	1	0
Michael Johnson	3	0	5	0	8	0
Gelson Fernandes	3 (14)	1	6 (4)	1	9 (18)	2
Dietmar Hamann	5 (4)	0	3 (6)	1	8 (10)	1
Vincent Kompany	34	0	10 (1)	1	44 (1)	1
Nigel de Jong	16	0	0	0	16	0
Stephen Ireland	33 (1)	9	14 (1)	4	47 (2)	13
Shaun Wright-Phillips	27	5	10	3	37	8
Elano	20 (8)	6	10 (4)	2	30 (12)	8
Martin Petrov	4 (5)	0	4 (1)	2	8 (6)	2
Kelvin Etuhu	2 (2)	0	0 (3)	0	2 (5)	0
Vladimir Weiss	0 (1)	0	0	0	0 (1)	0
Valeri Bojinov	2 (6)	1	0 (1)	0	2 (7)	1
Robinho	30 (1)	14	10	1	40 (1)	15

FINAL TABLE 2008/09

	P	W	D	L	F	A	W	D	L	F	A	Pts	GD
Man Utd	38	16	2	1	43	13	12	4	3	25	11	90	+44
Liverpool	38	12	7	0	41	13	13	4	2	36	14	86	+50
Chelsea	38	11	6	2	33	12	14	2	3	35	12	83	+44
Arsenal	38	11	5	3	31	16	9	7	3	37	21	72	+31
Everton	38	8	6	5	31	20	9	6	4	24	17	63	+18
Aston Villa	38	7	9	3	27	21	10	2	7	27	27	62	+6
Fulham	38	11	3	5	28	16	3	8	8	11	18	53	+5
Tottenham	38	10	5	4	21	10	4	4	11	24	35	51	0
West Ham	38	9	2	8	23	22	5	7	7	19	23	51	-3
Man City	38	13	0	6	40	18	2	5	12	18	32	50	+8
Wigan	38	8	5	6	17	18	4	4	11	17	27	45	-11
Stoke	38	10	5	4	22	15	2	4	13	16	40	45	-17
Bolton	38	7	5	7	21	21	4	3	12	20	32	41	-12
Portsmouth	38	8	3	8	26	29	2	8	9	12	28	41	-19
Blackburn	38	6	7	6	22	23	4	4	11	18	37	41	-20
Sunderland	38	6	3	10	21	25	3	6	10	13	29	36	-20
Hull	38	3	5	11	18	36	5	6	8	21	28	35	-25
Newcastle	38	5	7	7	24	29	2	6	11	16	30	34	-19
Middlesbro	38	5	9	5	17	20	2	2	15	11	37	32	-29
West Brom	38	7	3	9	26	33	1	5	13	10	34	32	-31

Summer**Signings**
ROQUE**SANTA**CRUZ

The Blackburn Rovers striker joined the Blues after Mark Hughes made him one of his top targets

Name: Roque Luis Santa Cruz Cantero **Born:** 16/08/1981
Age: 28 **Birthplace:** Asuncion, Paraguay **Position:** Striker

ROQUE Santa Cruz signed for City in July 2009. The Paraguayan international is a proven goal-scorer and, in many ways, an old fashioned centre forward who can be devastating in the air and is excellent at holding up the ball up and bringing others into play.

Mark Hughes knows exactly what he will get from the striker and went as far as to say that he believes the Blues would have qualified for the Europa League last season had a deal been agreed back in January.

The prospect of Santa Cruz up front with the likes of Carlos Tevez, Shaun Wright-Phillips and Robinho is a mouth-watering one for Blues fans – so what do we know about Santa Cruz? Well, he was born in August 1981 in the Paraguayan capital Asuncion – one of South America's oldest cities – and he joined his hometown club of Olimpia Asuncion at the age of 9!

Roque was invited to train with the senior squad at the age of 15 thanks to his fantastic goal-scoring record at youth level and within two years he had made his senior debut in what the Paraguayans call the 'Superclasico' match between Cerro Porten and Olimpia. Before his 18th birthday he had won two championship medals for Asuncion.

His star continued to rise rapidly with three goals at the FIFA World Youth Championships and, remarkably, still only 18, was called up for the Paraguay senior squad to play in the 1999 Copa America, scoring three times for his country. Hardly surprising then that he was later voted Paraguayan Footballer of the Year. With South American scouts abound, it was no great surprise

that this precocious talent should attract the attention of some of Europe's top clubs and in 1999 he joined German giants Bayern Munich.

His first-team opportunities were somewhat limited during his early days in Germany, though the club won the Bundesliga five times during his time there, four domestic cup competitions and the 2001 Champions League – not bad, but Roque wanted regular first team football and after 31 goals in 145 appearances for Bayern, then-Blackburn manager Mark Hughes came in with an offer of £3.5m for the player who would become an instant crowd favourite at Ewood Park.

After a magnificent first season with Blackburn, he quickly became the target of several top clubs in England and abroad and, inevitably, Hughes' move to City meant he was continually linked with a move to City, but he committed to Blackburn by penning a new four-year deal at Ewood Park.

Finally, after 23 goals in 57 appearances for Rovers, Santa Cruz agreed to become a Manchester City player in July 2009. On signing, he said "I'm very happy to have signed for City - it's been close to happening for a while, and now I can just focus on football and concentrate on doing my best for the club.
"I know the kind of football Mark Hughes wants to play and the kind of character he is - he's a winner, he wants to make things happen and be successful. I decided to come to City after I heard the fans talking about me on the radio – I liked their passion!
"I know the club is going in the right direction. I know his staff and the kind of training they will have the team doing, so everything was very attractive for me."

INFORMATIONDOWNLOAD:
CAREER HIGHLIGHTS:

• He will wear the No.24 shirt for the Blues
• At 6 feet 2.5 inches he is City's tallest senior striker
• He scored with just his third touch of the ball on his debut against Middlesbrough!
• He became the first player in 11 years to score a hat-trick in the top flight and still end up on the losing side with his treble against Wigan in vain during a 5-3 defeat
• His brother Julio joined him at Blackburn – sadly, another of Roque's brothers, Oscar, died
• Married to Giselle, the sister of his former national teammate Ricardo in 2003. They have a son, Tobias (born 17 December 2003), and a daughter, Fiorella (born 11 November 2005)
• In a 2006 FIFA World Cup edition of German magazine Kicker he was voted the most handsome man to be taking part in the tournament!

QuizAnswers

QUOTES QUIZ
(From page 25)

1. Chairman Khaldoon Al Mubarak – on Mark Hughes' future
2. Mark Hughes – pondering over City's UEFA Cup exit
3. Robinho – looking forward to silverware at City
4. Mark Hughes - trying to figure out why Pablo Zabaleta has been overlooked by Argentina coach Diego Maradona
5. Craig Bellamy – responding to criticism after Wales lose to Finland
6. Stephen Ireland – prior to signing a new, long-term contract
7. Robinho – mapping out a blueprint for the future
8. Craig Bellamy – getting with the project
9. Nigel de Jong – shortly after joining City
10. Mark Hughes – explaining why Carrington had to become a more private environment

WORDSEARCH
(From page 24)

WHO IS CELEBRATING?
(From page 34)

A) ROBINHO

B) SHAUN-WRIGHT-PHILLIPS

C) FELIPE CAICEDO

D) NEDUM ONUOHA

BIG CITY QUIZ - ANSWERS
(From page 30)

1 Leslie

2 Phil Brown (Hull City)

3 b) airline

4 Bolton

5 True – on loan!

6 Robinho, Elano & Danny Sturridge

7 Leeds United

8 Stephen Ireland, Felipe Caicedo & Robinho

9 Stephen Ireland – 35 seconds v Hamburg

10 Slovakia

11 b) 1998

12 FC Midtjylland and Aalborg

13 Spurs

14 Ched Evans

15 5-3

16 Oakwell, Barnsley

17 5

18 8 (Elano 5, Sturridge 1, Robinho 1 + 1 miss)

19 Basel (Switzerland)

20 Shaun Wright-Phillips (39)

21 16

22 Sunderland

23 False – the answer is five

24 Three

25 Diego

26 Nigeria

27 1 – Danny Califf v Midtjylland

28 Liverpool

29 Manchester United

30 Fulham

SPOT THE BALL (From page 45)

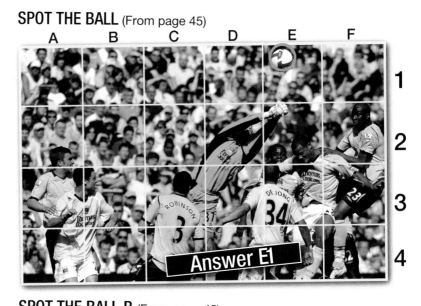

Answer E1

SPOT THE BALL B (From page 45)

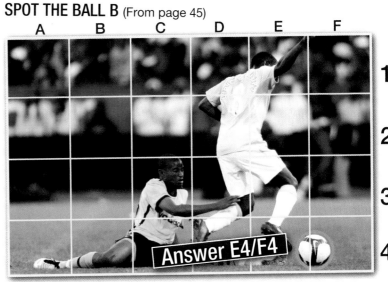

Answer E4/F4

CROSSWORD SOLUTION (From page 35)